THE LOW SKY

in pictures

UNDERSTANDING THE DUTCH THE BOOK THAT MAKES THE NETHERLANDS FEEL FAMILIAR

PHOTOGRAPHY FREEK VAN ARKEL GEORGE BURGGRAAFF BEN DEIMAN
ETIENNE VAN SLOUN | GREGOR RAMAEKERS KAREL TOMEÏ
TEXT HAN VAN DER HORST PUBLISHER SCRIPTUM

THE
LOW SKY

in pictures

1

'YOU SHOULD NOT STAY HERE,' Brazilian Dirceu Borges told his daughter on a short visit to the Netherlands, where she had made her home. 'The sky is too low.' Borges, was referring to the climate in all senses of the word. It wasn't just that he missed the open expanse of the firmament that, in the Netherlands, is more often than not concealed from view by rain clouds. He was also immediately impressed by the unending flatness of the land – and observed a corresponding effect on the mental and spiritual climate of the country.

What does it mean to be in the Netherlands? Creeping slowly forward on a motorway, looking through the swishing windscreen wipers at a horizon dotted with apartment blocks. The southwest wind is driving grey clouds across the sky at a speed that makes you envious.

'You should not stay here,' Brazilian Dirceu Borges told his daughter on a short visit to the Netherlands, where she had made her home. 'The sky is too low.' Borges, the prototype of an entrepreneur, was referring to the climate in all senses of the word. It wasn't just that he missed the open expanse of the firmament that, in the Netherlands, is more often than not concealed from view by rain clouds. He was also immediately impressed by the unending flatness of the land – and observed a corresponding effect on the mental and spiritual climate of the country. To Borges, the Dutch view of the world was determined by the low sky under which they lived and their flat country, all divided up neatly into geometric shapes, demarcated by canals and ditches. He missed an abundance of spiritual space and could not escape the impression that the desire for adventure had also been carefully fenced off.

Occasionally, the slowly moving traffic comes to a complete stop, giving non-Dutch drivers the opportunity to observe their fellow road-users. One thing is immediately clear – this is a very rich country. There are few old cars on the road, and a lot of trucks, all looking well maintained. They carry valuable cargo, mostly finished industrial products rather than raw materials. The many telephone numbers and e-mail addresses displayed on their doors and sides bear witness to a country which is well-advanced in the field of electronic communications and where the development of the electronic superhighway is in full swing. The other car drivers have taken advantage of the standstill to reach for their cell phones. Their calls are short. They are not calling their families, but are reporting in to work, most likely to say that they will be in a little later than planned.

THE MOST EXPENSIVE CARS
ARE MIDDLE-RANGE FAMILY MODELS

Yet this impression of extreme wealth may be somewhat misleading. In the heavy traffic on the motorway, there are a few very genuine luxury cars. Most are middle-range family models, with a large percentage of Asian origin, showing just how successful Oriental manufacturers have been in competing with their European counterparts. But the top end of the market is barely represented. There are no Rolls Royces, Cadillacs, Daimlers or Jaguars. Even in the country's business centres or elite residential areas, they are very few and far between. The best place to see the world's most exclusive cars in the Netherlands is at one of the few dealers who sells them. Generally speaking, the most expensive cars you see on the roads are standard German models from Mercedes Benz or BMW.

If you should see someone winding their way through the traffic in a Rolls Royce, you will notice that they command little respect. On the contrary, the middle-range drivers might even seem to be making life difficult for this symbol of opulence, as if they consider it offensive to appear in such a limousine on the public highway. The owners of the Renaults, Toyotas, Hyundais and Volkswagens will try and prove to this show-off in his Rolls Royce that they are every bit as good as he is. Anyone daring to take to the road in an exclusive motorcar will soon find that other road-users do their best to overtake him.

The countryside on each side of the motorway is interspersed with a large number of towns and villages. Real metropolises, with millions of people, do not exist in the Netherlands. The largest municipality has a population of no more than 700,000. Yet the Nether-

lands is the world's most highly urbanized country. Every few kilometres there will be a motorway exit, leading to two or three places with populations ranging from a few thousand to, at the most, a little over 100,000. The towns and villages all have their own character but there is rarely much to choose between them in terms of prosperity. There are no hovels, but no palaces either. The streets are lined with solid, dependable middle-class homes. Even Wassenaar, Aerdenhout or Rozendaal – the Dutch equivalents of Beverly Hills – are rather modest in international terms. They present an image of reliability and prosperity, but lack the glamour and glitter of big money.

The same is true of the country's yacht marinas. Anyone in the Netherlands who buys a pleasure yacht will have great difficulty finding a place to moor it, because most of them will already be occupied. But not by the kind of luxury three-masters with a permanent crew that can be seen, for example, in the resort of Angrea dos Reis in Brazil. Dutch marinas are full of motor and sailing boats of all kinds. But the ones that stand out, with a deeper draught or a higher mast, generally fly a foreign flag.

You might be excused for thinking that socialism had taken hold in the Netherlands, perhaps even more so than in the countries of the former Eastern bloc. But the economic statistics tell a very different story. In terms of per capita income, the Netherlands is one of the leaders in the European Union. After being severely hit by the second oil crisis in 1979, the country restored growth after five years and has continued to grow almost without interruption ever since. It is home to several multinational corporations of various sizes, notably the electronics concern Philips and banking giants RABO and ABN AMRO. In addition, there are Shell and Unilever, which are joint British-Dutch concerns. This means that there must be enormous quantities of wealth concentrated in the hands of a few individuals. And indeed, in a population of 16 million people there are more than 200,000 millionaires, a number which has grown considerably during the past decade. This is not so surprising, in a nation with an average income of $ 35,000 per head. Apparently, however, these wealthy people do not spend their money on palaces. And, apparently, very few of them feel the need to visit the Rolls Royce dealer.

THE DIRECTOR AND HIS HIRED DAIMLER

The Nolet distillery in the very Dutch town of Schiedam – 80,000 inhabitants, a lot of middle-class housing developments around a historical town centre – is a typical medium-sized Dutch company. Despite the presence of the multinationals and of many other large corporations, small and medium-size enterprise is still the cornerstone of the Dutch economy, and often of technical and commercial innovation. Nolet's products – high quality spirits – are very popular with Dutch consumers but, like many other companies of a similar size in the Netherlands, it is not afraid of the international market. The company boasts a prizewinning video film, especially made to introduce its products to wholesalers in the United States. In the film the director is seen driving in his Daimler. When it is shown to visitors to the company in the Netherlands, they are told that the car was hired for the day on the advice of the advertizing agency. In America, a classic car like the Daimler is proof that the company is established and trustworthy. This explanation is essential for Dutch

There are no hovels, but no palaces either. The streets are lined with solid, dependable middle-class homes. Even Wassenaar, Aerdenhout or Rozendaal – the Dutch equivalents of Beverly Hills – are rather modest in international terms. They present an image of reliability and prosperity, but lack the glamour and glitter of big money.

viewers, because they have a completely different response. If a company director drives a Daimler, he is obviously a little too fond of the good life. That's why the prices of his products are so high. Well, they think, we're not going to pay for him to drive around in a Daimler. What's more, this is a man who creams off the profits from his company instead of ploughing them back into the business. He is clearly not to be taken seriously and is best kept at a distance.

In 1997 a number of top managers awarded themselves substantial bonuses through a cleverly constructed share options plan. They thought that the annual figures of their companies were so high that they deserved a reward. The prime minister of the Netherlands at the time, Wim Kok, expressed his distaste of the plan in public. He said that the managers were 'greedy money-grabbers' and accused them of undermining his government's policy of moderation in price and salary increases, one of the secrets of Dutch economic success. And a majority of the public and the media agreed with him. A lifestyle of conspicuous consumption is counterproductive in the Netherlands. One of the most popular sayings in Dutch is *Doe gewoon, dan doe je gek genoeg* – Just act normally, that's crazy enough. Anyone who acts 'abnormally' generates opposition. And this is what Dirceu Borges understood so quickly, this was what he had meant by the low sky. He was afraid that, in such a well-ordered landscape as this, where you might be able to see a long way into the distance but not very far directly above, creativity itself may be forced into a straitjacket of 'normality'. Just as the fields and meadows have all been laid out in a neat pattern. It is all so terribly standardized. It gives the individual little opportunity to excel, to be anything more than average.

There is another Dutch saying that fosters this kind of mentality: *als je je hoofd boven het maaiveld uitsteekt, wordt het onmiddellijk afgehakt*. If you stick your head out above the rest, it will immediately be chopped off. You often hear this from people who are having little success in getting their plans and ideas put into practice. This, of course, can lead to the dangerous conclusion that most Dutch people are driven by jealousy. Sanctions await those who distinguish themselves in any way. Although this conclusion is understandable, it is also inaccurate. A nation driven by jealousy cannot build up a per capita income of $ 35,000. The reason must lie elsewhere.

The presence of so many small urban communities, while there are no large metropolises like Paris, Berlin, Bangkok or Tokyo, puts us on the right track. Another clue is the absence of large estates in the flat, neatly laid out countryside – so perfectly encapsulated in Dutch as *het platte land*, the 'flat land', even in the south and east,

where the landscape is more undulating. This is a country that has never known dominant power centres like Versailles or Peking's Forbidden City.

Even Amsterdam, the capital, plays a relatively modest role. It is the home of the Stock Exchange and the national printed media. And anyone seeking to make a name in the arts will be well advised to head for the canaldistrict in the old city centre. But the national government and parliament are to be found in The Hague. The broadcasting media have settled in Hilversum. Rotterdam is the largest port in the country (and in the world), while Utrecht is the leading centre for conferences and other large-scale events. The Netherlands in effect has several 'capitals'. Amsterdam was only designated as the official national capital in 1806, by Louis Napoleon, a usurper placed in power by his brother, the French emperor. After the fall of the Bonapartes, the city retained its status.

Anyone delving into the history of the Netherlands will find no great rulers or mighty champions of national unity, like Louis xiv or the Number One Emperor of China, or at least none who have ever had any great degree of success in these endeavours. The great historical figures in Dutch history have been liberators and conciliators.

THE CALVINIST MENTALITY IS STILL STRONG

In medieval times, the territory of what is now the Netherlands was covered by several counties and a small number of duchies. In the second half of the sixteenth century, as the culmination of a long-drawn-out historical process, they were all inherited by the King of Spain. He discovered that he was considerably restricted in the exercise of his power by the many privileges that had been acquired by towns and rural communities in the time of the counts and dukes. This amounted to a complex system of autonomy and regulations, by which the ruler was obliged to choose local administrators from a list of nominees drawn up by powerful families.

Philip ii, however, intended to put an end to this system of privileges. For the period, he was a very modern ruler, who believed in a strong central authority which imposed the same rules throughout the kingdom and whose ethical and ideological base was founded on a single, official religion, Catholicism. In the Netherlands, however, there was much support for Protestantism, particularly as preached by John Calvin. There was consequently considerable resistance to Philip ii, which eventually led to a successful revolt. One of the leading figures in the uprising was Wiliam of Orange, the founding father of the current Royal Family. William was a *stadhouder*, the official representative of the King in one of the counties,

Holland. But he could not accept the erosion of the traditional system of privileges and particularly the persecution of the Protestants, which was one of the main elements of Philip's strategy.

The revolt against Philip ii led to the setting up of the Republic of the United Provinces, based largely on the old privileges and the principle of local autonomy. It was in fact an alliance between separate states, in which the individual members also formed a federation, like the Commonwealth of Independent States set up after the fall of the Soviet Union. Within such an alliance, any member who blew his own trumpet too loudly or gave any outward display of power or wealth ran the risk of a coalition being formed against him. No one could amass sufficient power to become dominant in the new Republic. High position depended on influence, not on might. This also applied to the stadholders, who were always from the family of Orange and who succeeded in making the position hereditary. They had the power formerly exercised by Philip ii, but were limited by the countless privileges and traditional rights of the old system.

The only way to achieve anything in the Republic was to form coalitions and to do so without overly offending your opponents. Respect for others, a modest lifestyle, a willingness to listen and a capacity for restraint, in all senses of the word, were the secret of success. Calvinism, which was embraced – albeit in a rather liberal form – by a significant part of the elite, had a considerable effect on this view of the world. John Calvin's philosophy had much in common with a cloudy sky. Man is by nature evil, said Calvin. He can attain salvation only by the mercy of God. As the descendant of Adam, driven out of Paradise, man shall eat bread in the sweat of his face. To enjoy is a sign of pride and to invoke the Devil. And there is always the threat of the punishing hand of the Almighty.

The Netherlands has not been an alliance of states for a long time. It is now a democratic state, the unity of which is symbolized by a Queen who descends from William of Orange. But the mentality remains essentially unchanged. To flaunt one's wealth shows a lack of respect, not only for one's fellow man, but also for God. And, even in the strongly secularized society of the end of the twentieth century, many Dutch people still believe that this is to tempt fate unnecessarily.

The countryside on each side of the motorway is interspersed with a large number of towns and villages. Real metropolises, with millions of people, do not exist in the Netherlands. The largest municipality has a population of no more than 730,000. Yet the Netherlands is the world's most highly urbanized country. Every few kilometres there will be a motorway exit, leading to two or three places with populations ranging from a few thousand to, at the most, a little over 100,000. The towns and villages all have their own character but there is rarely much to choose between them in terms of prosperity.

2

To live on land that has been 'snatched from the sea', gives a great feeling of confidence. If the land itself is 'makable', can be formed by the hand of man, then other areas of reality may also prove to be so – society, for example. As long as it is founded on good organization and close cooperation, of course.

YOU CAN ONLY WORK WITH THE WATER, NOT AGAINST IT

'God created Heaven and Earth, but the Dutch created the Netherlands.' You will rarely hear the Dutch say this of themselves, but they like to hear it from foreigners. It is always a good way to win them over if you have been asked to address a Dutch audience.

The impression this saying creates of the Netherlands is only partly reflected in reality. No more than a third of the country would actually fall prey to the waters of the North Sea and the major rivers, if they were not held at bay by dykes and other testaments to Dutch ingenuity in hydraulic engineering. The rest would stay high and dry without them.

On the other hand, the majority of the population lives in areas protected by dunes and dykes. The largest cities and the most important industrial areas are to be found in the west of the country, which is essentially a river delta, like those of the Nile, the Ganges, the Mekong and the Mississippi. So, while you are making your speech it might not go amiss to say a few words about the eternal battle against the water in the Netherlands. And about how, after terrible defeats – like the disastrous floods in February 1953, when almost 2,000 people lost their lives – the battle was finally won. This victory is best expressed in the Delta Project, a line of enormous dykes and sluices, which prevent the tempestuous sea from forcing its way up into the river estuaries. The Delta defences are designed to withstand a combination of storms and a spring tide so awesome that it is calculated to occur only once every 10,000 years. But – as all Dutch people know – that can be tomorrow.

This indeed creates the impression of a permanent war against the water, which is at best interrupted on occasion by ceasefires or by endless siege. But the reality is a little more complicated. The Dutch do not actually fight the water. They know there is no point in doing so, because it is invincible. Nothing can withstand its power. They therefore have a kind of symbiotic relationship with the water. At most they have persuaded the gigantic forces of nature to accommodate themselves somewhat to the needs of man. Because you can only work with the water, not against it. A cold war you might be able to keep up for some time. But when it comes to open warfare, you are lost from the start.

THE WOMEN WORE JEWELLERY OF SILVER AND GOLD

This implicit understanding is based on the experience of several thousand years. At the beginning of the modern era, the delta of the four major rivers – the Scheldt, Maas, Rhine and Eems – the area now covered by the Netherlands, was already inhabited. Behind the line of dunes that marked the coastline, in flat marshlands crisscrossed by countless streams, farmers had here and there constructed artificial mounds. Many of these flat-topped mounds are still to be seen, particularly in the provinces of Friesland and Groningen. Here, the farmers lived together with their cattle, which grazed on the surrounding mud flats and salt marshes. When there was a danger of excessively high water – there was always plenty of warning; hurricane-force storms are a rarity in a country with a normally temperate climate – they would gather all their cattle together and take refuge on the mounds. The Roman writer Pliny the Elder devoted a few sympathetic paragraphs to the sufferings of these people, whom he saw as leading a pitiful existence at the mercy of ruthless natural forces. But archeological finds suggest a different picture. The cattle farmers in the delta region 2,000 years ago had relatively large herds, often with fifty or more animals. The women wore jewellery of silver and gold, which must have been even more costly for having to be brought in from afar.

But research tells us even more. The power of the sea has been steadily increasing over the past few thousand years. This is due to long-term climatological changes which have been accompanied by

a gradual melting of the polar caps. One result of these changes was that the bogs and marshes were under water for an increasing number of days each year. The response to this was an invention that still forms the basis of all Dutch hydraulic engineering works, the *duiker*. A *duiker* is a pipe with a hinged flap at the end. As the tide comes in it closes automatically and opens again as the water recedes. No one knows when this simple contraption was first introduced, but there is a strong suspicion that the Romans may have been behind it.

Thanks to the *duiker* it became possible to enclose areas of land with dykes, embankments of earth. The *duikers* would keep the water out as level rose, and allow it to drain out again as it retreated. It was also necessary to dig a network of drainage ditches in the land enclosed by the dykes. This simple system proved effective until well into the Middle Ages, but then the power of the sea had increased to such an extent that the *duikers* were no longer able to cope. Fortunately a new innovation was imported from the Islamic world – the windmill. A large windmill could generate about as much power as a modern-day middle-range motorcar. With the aid of paddle wheels and – from the end of the sixteenth century – the Archimedes' screw, it was once again possible to drain all the excess water. If one windmill was not enough, several were linked together in parallel, as can still be seen today at Kinderdijk, near Rotterdam. The combination of dykes and windmill-powered drainage enabled most of the country behind the dunes to be drained and kept dry. The number of present-day place names containing the words *meer* (lake) and *plas* (pond) bear witness to a time when much of the delta was still at the mercy of the water.

Since the nineteenth century the windmills have gradually been replaced by mechanically-operated pumps. Initially, they were driven by steam and later by diesel or electric motors. But no matter how modern the technology, the basic principle is the same as that of the *duiker* – even in the colossal structures of the Delta Works.

A DYKE IS ONLY AS STRONG AS ITS WEAKEST POINT
A piece of land enclosed by dykes is known in Dutch as a *polder*. No one can say for certain what the etymological origins of the word are, and other languages do not have a suitable equivalent. Polders come in all shapes and sizes, from a few hectares to tens of thousands. The largest, the eastern part of the province of Flevoland, covers 48,000 hectares. What does it cost to maintain all these polders? Somewhere between three and three and a half billion guilders a year – not too much of a problem for a country with a national income of 375 billion guilders.

The management of a polder demands close cooperation from its users. Originally, it was the responsibility of those who lived on dykes to maintain them. This, however, meant that those living in the middle of the polder enjoyed the protection without having to earn it. This unfair situation was later replaced by one in which all the inhabitants shared responsibility for the maintenance of the dykes, *duikers* and, later, the windmills. At first, the head of each family was designated a piece of the dyke which he had to maintain according to very detailed rules and regulations. The penalties for failing to do so were typically medieval in their cruelty. Later, dykes and drainage systems also became communal projects. A complete hierarchy of specialized functions evolved, with a corresponding bureaucracy – the water boards. These boards, with their own powers and the authority to levy taxes, still exist today. For the past few decades, they have been responsible not only for protecting the land inside the dykes, but also for the quality of the water, which has been severely affected by pollution.

It was once believed that Dutch democracy had its roots in the cooperation that was needed to survive in the polders, but this was a misconception. The system was in fact very authoritarian in the beginning and it was only later that landowners themselves managed to exert any influence on policy. Life behind the dykes definitely had a very profound impact on Dutch society, but it did not turn the Dutch into democrats. A far more likely legacy is their love of detailed agreements that have to be kept to the letter. In the polders, the smallest of errors, each little inaccuracy, can potentially mean disaster. A dyke is only as strong as its weakest point. All those involved in maintenance and drainage must therefore know their tasks and responsibilities down to the smallest detail. They must also coordinate their activities exactly with those of their colleagues, so that the entire human machine runs like clockwork. To keep the polder dry, you have to be able to depend on each other. In Dutch society, therefore, reliability is a great virtue and is always one of the main selection criteria when assessing job applications. Anyone with an eye for detail without losing sight of the big picture also commands great respect in the Netherlands.

And that is not all. To live on land that has been 'snatched from the sea', to use an expression the Dutch themselves favour, gives a great feeling of confidence. If the land itself is 'makable', can be formed by the hand of man, then other areas of reality may also prove to be so – society, for example. As long as it is founded on good organization and close cooperation, of course. When you know that you are safe behind the dyke, because of the efforts of successful engineers, it is a small step to believe in the beneficial effects of social engineering. "Economics is actually an engineering science," said

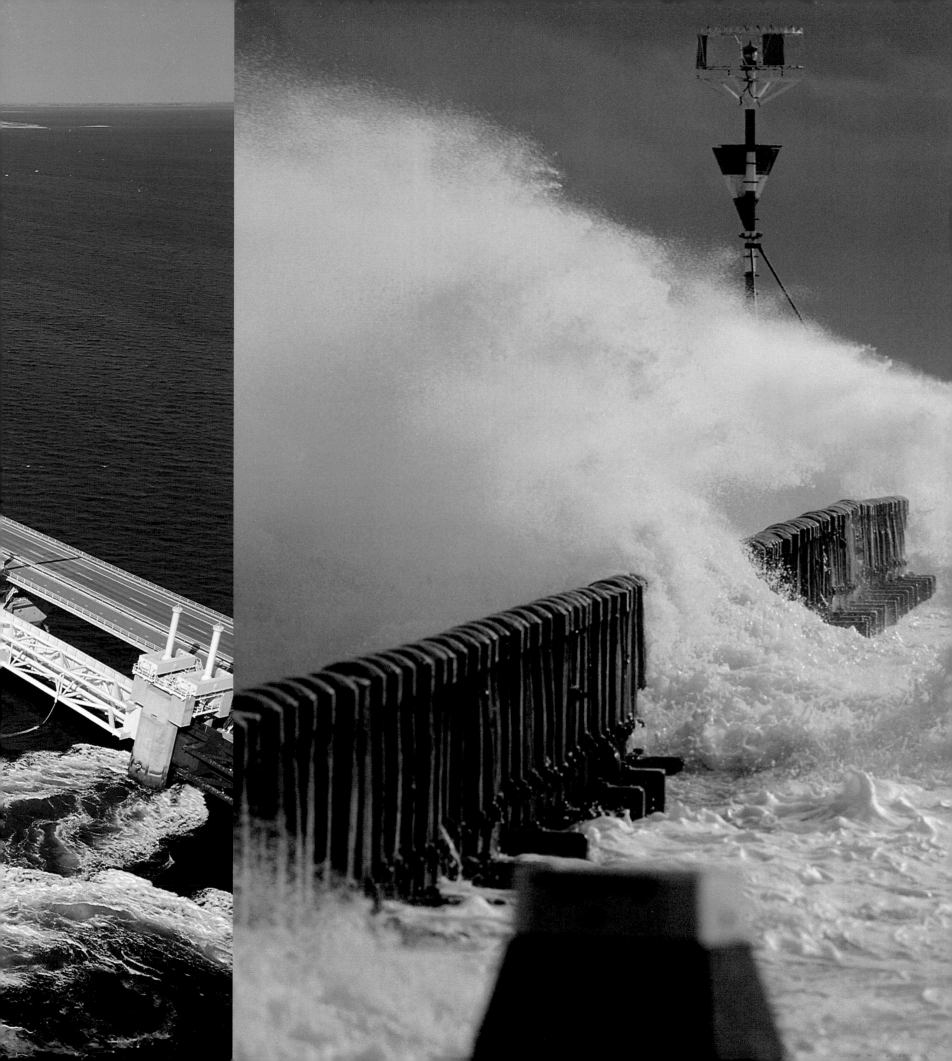

Professor Jan Tinbergen, who won the Nobel Prize for laying the foundations of econometrics.

Foreigners are always struck by the advanced degree of organization and planning in Dutch society. Everything is agreed and arranged. Nothing is left to coincidence. There are detailed norms and instructions for all eventualities. Anyone who puts up a shed in their garden without permission, to indulge in some traditional craft or other, will soon find the authorities on his back because it does not comply with the *bestemmingsplan*, the zoning plan in which the use of every building in the municipality is designated. This is difficult to accept for someone who can look out of his window and see a group of kids with cell phones further up the street, who are most likely selling drugs while the police seem to do nothing to stop them.

This, too, is related to what you learn from living behind the dyke. It is no easy task to drain land, dam rivers or try to alter their courses. Anyone who turns their back on the water completely, is risking complete inundation. You can only regulate the water if you continue to show respect for its primal power. The way that power is harnessed will vary according to the situation and will have to take account of the specific conditions. There is no theory, model or template that is applicable in all circumstances. The 'makability' is not founded on a system, but on a network of specific practical solutions which you hope will together generate sufficient added value. Some forces simply cannot be contained, only regulated so as to minimize the negative consequences. This is known in the Netherlands as *gedogen*, roughly the equivalent of the word 'tolerance' in English.

Some undesirable social phenomena cannot be eradicated with legal measures and the threat of punishment. On the contrary, they can develop into a countervailing force with the potential to damage the fabric of society as a whole. It is therefore better to restrict the damage to acceptable proportions by containing the problem within what you might call 'social dykes'. With this reasoning in mind, major Dutch cities have for many years had reception centres – known as *huiskamers*, 'living rooms' – where hard drugs users can take a breather. They can exchange their dirty needles for sterile ones, because the Netherlands prefers to have addicts without AIDS. The centres also make it easier for rehabilitation workers to recruit addicts for their programmes.

Nevertheless the use of both hard and soft drugs is still illegal. The authorities focus their attention on the fight against the large criminal organizations that control the worldwide trade in narcotics. There are frequent media reports of large consignments of smuggled drugs being intercepted, usually in the port of Rotterdam. As Europe's leading transit country, the Netherlands is attractive for criminal organizations, which try to make illicit use of the many global transport networks that pass through Dutch territory. A clampdown on addicts and small-scale dealers would only force them underground, where they would no longer be accessible to care workers. At the same time, the government funds permanent campaigns to inform young people of the dangers of addiction. This strategy has been a success. Studies have shown that the average age of cocaine and heroin addicts is increasing, a sign that the drugs have little attraction for the younger generation. The average addict is now in his late thirties and support organizations are already preparing for the problems of caring for elderly addicts. The number of people addicted to hard drugs in the Netherlands, with its population of 16 million, is around 25,000.

There is no point in fighting the water, because it is invincible. Nothing can withstand its power. The Delta defences are designed to withstand a combination of storms and a spring tide so awesome that it is calculated to occur only once every 10,000 years. But – as all Dutch people know – that can be tomorrow.

THE POLDER MODEL

Anyone who asks on what principle this policy of tolerance is based will rarely receive an answer. It is the result of a series of practical solutions for specific problems. This can affect the nature and intensity of the solutions. In spite of the success of the policy of tolerance in keeping the problem of hard drugs addiction within manageable bounds, many authorities now wonder whether they may not at times have been too tolerant.

In another area that has caused social problems, prostitution, tolerance has given way to legalization. Since 1911, the Netherlands had decency laws that forbade the practice of offering the services of a prostitute. It was permitted for women to sell their own bodies, but pimps and brothel owners were guilty of a criminal offence. The law has never been applied to the letter. It was used by the authorities to restrict prostitution to certain districts and streets in the major cities, which had already had a bad reputation for many years. This made it easier for the police to keep an eye on the situation and ensure that the brothels did not use under-age girls. They were also able to keep violent or criminal elements out of circulation.

But now, all brothels are to be legalized. Under the new laws, the central government and local authorities have to draw up detailed rules and regulations, largely aimed at protecting women who work as prostitutes from being exploited by the powerful 'kings' of the sex industry. Legalization will make it a lot easier to combat abuse. The holes and weak points in the dyke can be strengthened. And if the results are more disappointing than expected, other solutions will be sought to minimize the harmful effects of this unenviable profession.

In these and other areas, Dutch society chooses a policy of give and take, so that it can keep its feet dry, both literally and figuratively. In 1997, the British press devised a name for this method of living together: the polder model.

APPOINTMENTS ARE MADE TO BE KEPT

3

Making clear agreements and committing them to paper has become second nature in a country where decision-making is always a compromise between equal partners and where you have to be able to rely on each other if the water level rises too high.

PLAYING SAFE

The Netherlands has a very strong position on the international market. This is not because Dutch entrepreneurs offer their products at the lowest prices, which is not always possible in a rich country with high salaries and costly social services.

The secret is an optimal ratio between quality and price. And a reliability that has become legendary. Dutch companies supply their products exactly according to the specifications and exactly on time. Not too late, and not too early.

Daily life in the Netherlands offers countless examples of this mentality. At bus stops, the timetable tells you the bus times to the minute: 18.06, 17.46, 19.08, and so on. This is not a declaration of intent, but a target that the bus companies make every effort to meet. If the bus is delayed, the mood of the passengers waiting at the stop rapidly drops below zero. They look worriedly at their watches. They start to pace up and down impatiently. They reach for their cell phones. And when the bus finally arrives, perhaps five minutes late, the bus company knows it has a black mark against its name.

The passengers' reactions are less exaggerated than they may seem. Arriving on time and keeping appointments are important cornerstones of everyday life in the Netherlands. Now that the bus is late, they might miss their tram or train connection, compounding the delay. This causes problems not only for themselves, but also for those who may be waiting for them. They will not be able to devote the allotted time to the appointment and that upsets the planning for the rest of the day. For this reason it is also inadvisable to turn up at a Dutch company or other organization unexpectedly.

Often, after having made it clear that you do not have an appointment, you will not even make it past the reception. If you are lucky enough to get through to the person you wish to see, they will most likely give an irritated or abrupt impression, continually looking at their watch and clearly trying to bring the conversation to a close as soon as possible. They will make no attempt to stand on ceremony

and show little respect for your status. They will produce a diary to make a proper appointment with this intruder – for this is exactly what you are. As the diary lies open on the desk you can see that it is stuffed full with appointments and other notes. Here and there you will see a blank line. These are known as 'holes in the diary'. An appointment will be made to fill up one of these 'holes'. The time will be very exact, for example between 16.20 and 16.45. The probability of it being on the same day is very small. It is more likely to be days or weeks in the future. Often, it is very difficult to fix a date for a meeting months in advance because, every time a suggestion is made, at least one of the participants will 'already have an appointment' at that time.

APPOINTMENTS ARE MADE TO BE KEPT

This system works surprisingly well and efficiently, if everyone sticks to the rules. In other words, make an appointment for everything. Make sure others who you wish to meet do the same thing. And then keep to the appointments you have made. Because meetings are limited in duration, there is little time for pleasantries before getting down to the business in hand. The Dutch have no problem with this at all, and waste no time trying to form an impression of the person they are dealing with. To do so is even considered a little impolite. The Dutch keep their work and their private life strictly separate. They can take this to extremes. Business competitors may be close friends outside the office. And there are well-known examples of politicians happily married to colleagues from parties with diametrically opposing political views. Why this strict separation is maintained is explained in a later chapter. It is important here, in that it is part of what the Dutch themselves call their 'diary society'.

Making clear agreements and committing them to paper has become second nature in a country where decision-making is always a compromise between equal partners and where you have to be able to rely on each other if the water level rises too high. But the connection between these historical characteristics and the current fixation with time is not an obvious one. It is a relatively recent phenomenon. In the days of Rembrandt and Frans Hals, the Dutch were not at all punctual. There was no need to be. Life in the country was determined by the seasons. Work started at dawn and ceased at dusk, when the encroaching darkness made it impossible to continue, because the only form of lighting was flickering oil lamps. Only the rich could afford wax candles. During the summer, the working day was longer than in the winter. The situation was not so different in the towns. People earned a living in trade, fishing or

traditional crafts. Everyone had their own job to do and there was little need to coordinate their activities with those around them. That would not even have been possible, at least not until the Dutch inventor Christiaan Huygens discovered the secrets of the pendulum and used his new knowledge to build an accurate timepiece. Before this innovation, church bells would chime at different times of the day, telling everyone that it was time for lunch or that the town gates were to be closed. These chimes still ring out above the rooftops in many historical towns, but few of the inhabitants still know what they meant. At the time, the chiming of the bells was enough, because the lives of the townspeople did not need to be synchronized.

THE INDUSTRIAL REVOLUTION

This all changed when mechanization arrived. The industrial revolution started in the Netherlands around 1870 and changed the whole face of society within a few decades. Traditional workshops were replaced by factories driven by steam engines and, from the end of the nineteenth century, combustion engines and electric motors.

The new machinery created uniform, standardized products, such as rolls of textiles all with the same pattern, or components for other machines, which were assembled on another mechanically driven line. In these factories, the pace of the work was no longer determined by the workers, as in the old workshops, but by the machines. Once the steam engine was in operation, everyone had to be at their workplace and stay there until it stopped again. If someone was missing, the whole process would grind to a halt. That required a form of discipline that a society does not adapt to so easily. The founders of modern Dutch industry therefore had great difficulty imposing this mentality on their workers. Many investments failed because the workforce proved incapable of working to such tight schedules. They simply couldn't do it. It took several generations for the average Dutch employee to adapt to this new way of working.

Anyone wanting to be anywhere on time, must know what time it is. Thanks to the industrial revolution, cheap clocks became widely available and the alarm clock, with its rattling bells, soon became a fixture next to every bed. Local authorities placed public clocks liberally on the streets, and the conditions were created for everyone to know exactly what time it was at every hour of the day or night. If the Dutch now speak of someone 'knowing what the time is', it is a tribute to their common sense.

Around the same time, mass lighting made its entrance. Thanks to the invention of the lamp glass, evenly distributed artificial light became available at low cost. As gas companies offered an alternative to the oil lamp, the latter became cheaper and affordable for more and more people. The electric light bulb – initially the main product of Philips, a small company from Eindhoven that attracted international attention when it was contracted to provide the

Make an appointment for everything. Make sure others who you wish to meet do the same thing. And then keep to the appointments you have made. Because meetings are limited in duration, there is little time for pleasantries before getting down to the business in hand. The Dutch have no problem with this at all, and waste no time trying to form an impression of the person they are dealing with.

scale, the day often begins in the country's primary schools with a class discussion, during which the children are encouraged to talk about their own experiences and to express their opinions. Creativity and self-sufficiency do not necessarily mean eccentricity and obstinacy.

THE FATE OF THE ARTISTS

This high degree of organization, and faith in agreements, written procedures and fixed norms can clash with the free flow of ideas and impede creativity. The inbred mentality of the first industrial revolution, a mistrust of grand schemes and abstract theories, led to a desire to channel creativity, in a sense to enclose it with dykes. To say of someone that they have 'both feet on the ground' is a great compliment. Anyone who seems unable to control their flights of fancy is often accused of being footloose. 'When society is orderly, a fool alone cannot disturb it; when society is chaotic, a sage alone cannot bring order.' Many Dutch people would agree with this Taoist saying. Perhaps too readily. Those who place themselves too far outside the accepted limits soon find themselves isolated. This is frequently the fate of artists.

In the eyes of most Dutch people, artists are very special people who have a talent that few are privileged to possess. They should be cherished and protected. In a certain way, Dutch society still blames itself for not discovering Vincent van Gogh during his lifetime, sparing him the misery of committing suicide alone and penniless in a mental institution. This well organized society will not make the same mistake again. In the Netherlands, the government therefore supports artists. In the 1970s and 1980s there was even a system under which anyone who had graduated from art college, and was therefore a 'professional' artist, received an income from the government in exchange for a few pieces of work a year. The works were assessed by a committee of experts. These days the government believes that artists' fortunes are also better left to market forces, but young starters still receive a grant in their first few years to help them make a name for themselves.

There is, however, little genuine interaction between Dutch culture and everyday life. Literary commentators can write as many novels or essays as they like, and turn out best-sellers by the barrel load, but they will never become serious opinion leaders, as is the case in France, for example. Their social critique is, however, rewarded with grants and national prizes. The life of Multatuli – the pen name for Edward Douwes Dekker, the country's greatest writer and literary innovator of the nineteenth century – was a typical example. Multatuli was held in the highest esteem. His most famous work,

Max Havelaar, a fierce attack on the Netherlands' colonial policy, became a bestseller. His collections of essays were soon sold out, as were lecture halls – in spite of the high price of admission – wherever he appeared to speak. Key figures from the bourgeoisie formed committees to help him out of financial dire straits and to enable him to concentrate on his writing. His portraits were sold in bookshops. But when he stood as a candidate for parliament, he received only a few hundred votes.

On the other hand, artists themselves have little to do with the world of practical solutions. When well-known poet and literary critic Aad Nuis became state secretary for culture after a couple of terms in parliament, his popularity fell among his fellow artists, rather than their welcoming the fact that culture policy was, at last, in the hands of a colleague. No, the Netherlands is not a society in which an André Malraux, prominent literary innovator and Gaullist minister for culture, can thrive.

NO INVENTORS OR INNOVATORS

All of this has resulted in the Dutch having little talent for spectacular invention or innovation. They are not great lovers of fresh starts or of revolutions, even though they may use the word to describe something particularly new or a significant improvement to an existing product. This means that they are reliable managers, but not daring entrepreneurs. Parents with ambitions for their children hope that they will find a managerial position in a sound, established company, preferably a multinational, rather than set up their own business. The Dutch are by nature practically minded and adaptable.

Thanks to their precision and their attention to detail, they are very good at adapting to different circumstances and coming up with feasible solutions and alternatives. Those who seek their fortune elsewhere are successful as immigrants, fitting quickly into their new surroundings. They are also good at modifying their products to suit the requirements of foreign markets. Now that international services account for an increasing share of the gross national product, this gives them the edge over their competitors.

Yet they sometimes have problems with their well-ordered diary-driven society, seeing it as a straitjacket. They readily admit to foreign guests that it is a form of terrorism. They will take out their diaries and show you how ridiculous it all is. They will avidly claim to miss the grand gesture, and applaud speakers at congresses and seminars who call for innovation and creative solutions. They criticize their politicians and captains of industry for their lack of daring, even though the annual figures of the average company either belie this claim of over-cautiousness (or confirm it in no uncertain terms). But, when it comes down to it, the Dutch prefer to play it safe. They are great savers, in spite of the attempts of most banks to instil them with a love of consumptive credit. They will take out a loan, but only to buy a house or some other durable good, such as a car.

There is a famous Dutch poem that starts 'I wish my life to be grand and dramatic', only to be followed by: 'But not today. I think I'll wait a while'.

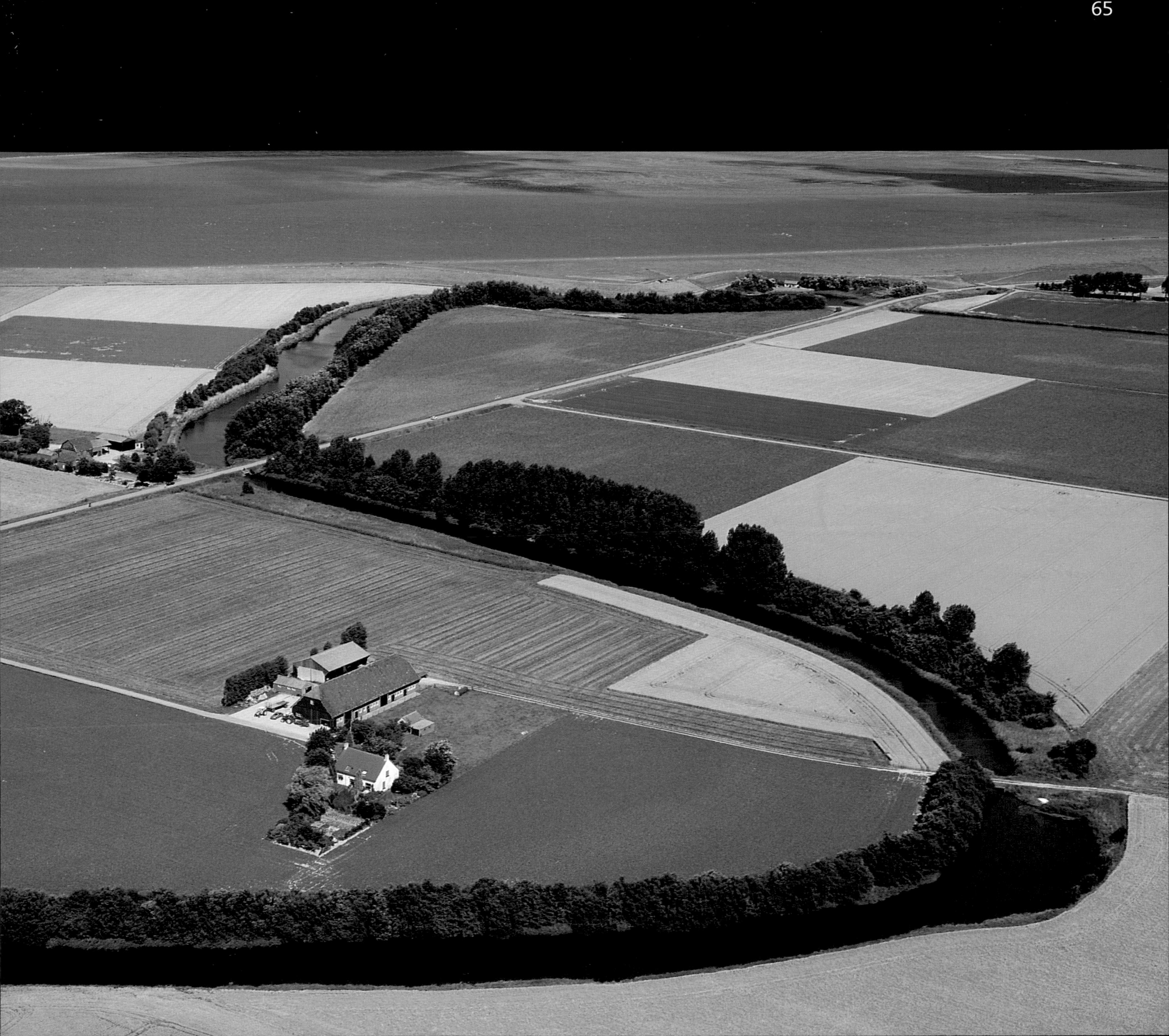

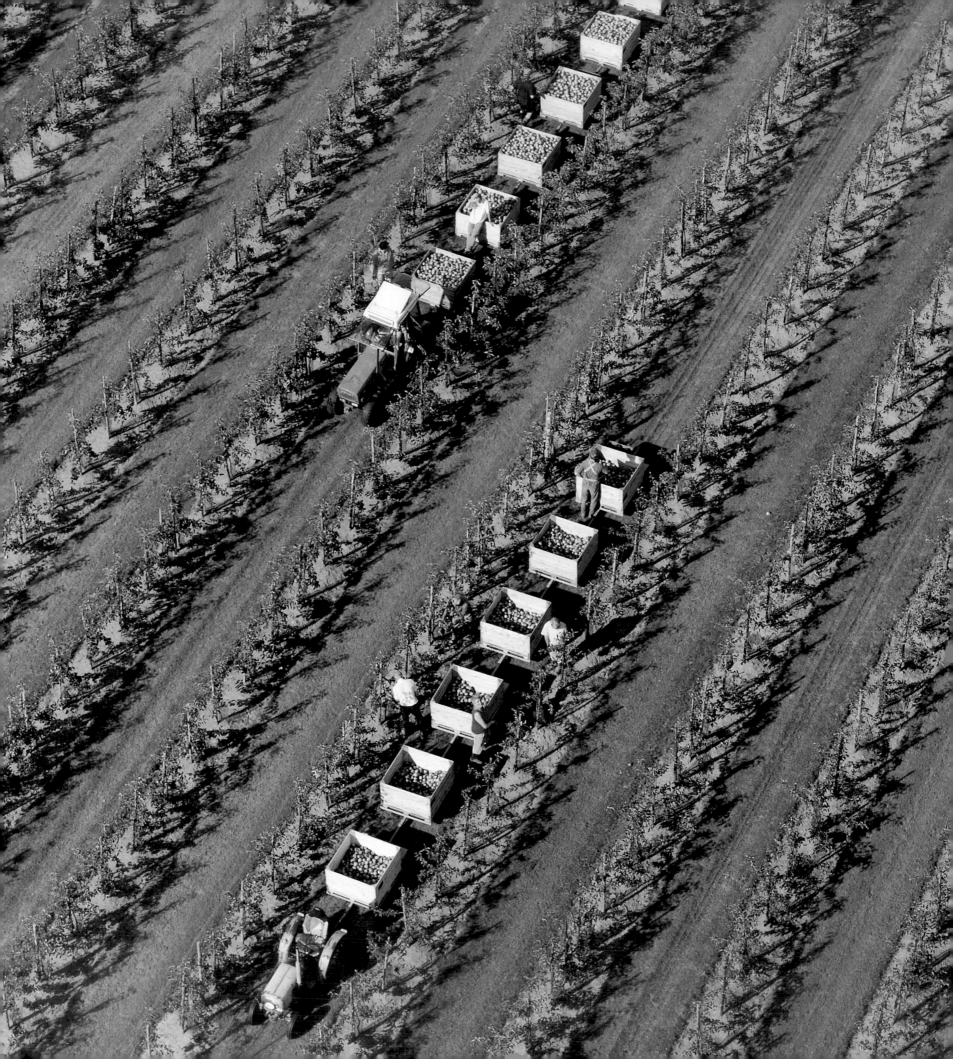

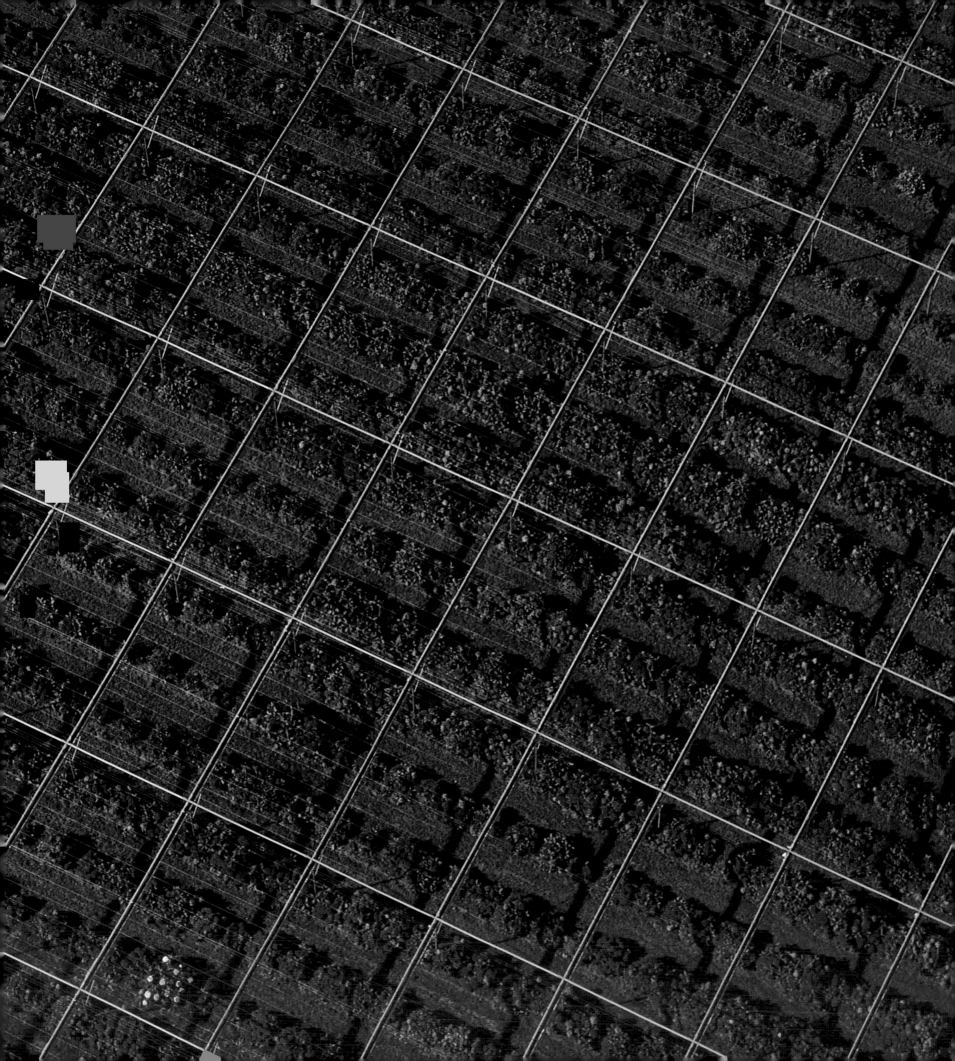

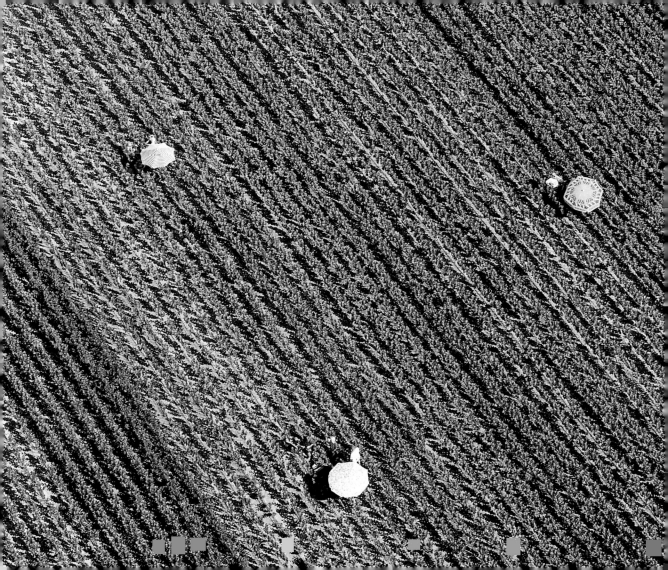

IF A DUTCH CAPTAIN OF INDUSTRY allows himself to be interviewed, he (or she, in the not so distant future) will try to play down his central role. He will claim that he is a team player and praise the creativity that is present in the whole company. He will insist that the company's success is down to everyone pulling together and that, without their boundless efforts, he would have been able to achieve nothing.

LEADERS LIKE TO STAY IN THE BACKGROUND

Not a year passes without historians or the more intellectual journalists complaining that prominent Dutch figures do not write their memoirs. Or, if they do, that they contain nothing of note.

Readers are treated to a description of recent history, with here and there an outline of the author's career. If they ever reveal their motives or their souls, this is rarely more than what Dutch captains of industry or leading politicians like to call a 'helicopter-view'. And even then, the helicopter in question is looking down from an unusually great height.

The Netherlands has no one like Lee Iaccoca. There are, of course, a large number of entrepreneurs who are capable of taking a company suffering from crisis and mismanagement firmly in hand and leading it through the recovery process with vision and verve. But they do not then tell the world about their feats in a bestseller. There have been recent instances of journalists daring to write the biography of a captain of industry, such as Freddy Heineken, the uncrowned emperor – to call him a king is simply not grand enough – of Dutch beer brewers. But then the subject does not cooperate on the project. The Dutch tend to be successful in secret, unless their careers are conducted amongst the stardust and glitter of Aalsmeer and Hilversum, the homes of the electronic media, which model themselves more and more on Hollywood.

This humility is unfortunate. It means that men who are of the greatest importance to Dutch society remain, through their own insistence, in the shadows. And they are indeed mostly men. Women only started to challenge for high positions about thirty years ago. They have had to overcome many obstacles and prejudices in their march to the top, which means that they are now fairly well represented at middle-management level, but are still a rarity on Boards of Directors. The only female captain of industry of international significance is Sylvia Toth, who took a medium-sized employment agency and built it up into a multinational. In 1998, she passed the baton on – to a man.

In this context, however, it is more interesting to address the question of why leaders in the Netherlands prefer to stay in the background and what consequences this has for anyone who wants to guide a company or organization safely through the storms of time. The phenomenal national income and the large number of Dutch or partially Dutch multinationals suggest that there is no shortage of talent in this respect. In addition to the obvious examples, like Philips, Shell or Unilever, there are less well-known but equally excellent companies, such as Enraf-Nonius, a world leader in aids for the handicapped, including wheelchairs and artificial limbs.

What would have become of Lee Iaccoca if Chrysler had been a Dutch company? His bestseller about how he saved a company that is one of the showpieces of American industry has enhanced his international reputation as an entrepreneur. In the Netherlands, such a book would lead only to raised eyebrows. He forgot to mention they would be saying around the drinks tables in the exclusive clubs, how he walks on water every day. He is a boaster, who attributes all his successes to himself. The book would do as much damage to the reputation of a Dutch Iaccoca as a Rolls Royce or a Cadillac under his illustrious rear end.

A TEAM PLAYER

If a Dutch captain of industry allows himself to be interviewed, he (or she, in the not so distant future) will try to play down his central role. He will claim that he is a team player and praise the creativity that is present in the whole company. He will insist that the company's success is down to everyone pulling together and that, without their boundless efforts, he would have been able to achieve nothing. He will not present himself as the genius with all the ideas, just as a coordinator. No matter that everyone involved knows that, without him, the company would long ago have disappeared from the stock listings.

This has everything to do with the great value the Dutch attach to equality and their general distaste for anything that is imposed upon them without their first being consulted. And, of course, with the actual need in so many cases to seek a compromise. But that is not all. Orders and commands are not easily digested by a people with an inbred belief in each individual's right to make up their own mind. These days, you often hear people say that they 'recognize themselves' in a decision, meaning that they were involved in the decision-making process. So when ministers or members of a Board of Directors choose to take a low profile, it is therefore a matter of strategy or tact.

Foreigners who come into contact with Dutch companies – either as customers or as employees – are often confused by all this. They are amazed at the informal way in which top-level managers and those lower down the scale interact. Secretaries address their bosses by their first names. There is little to suggest that the organization has a hierarchy. The managers' offices are simply furnished, as are the reception areas for visitors. It is not at all abnormal for the boss to join the lunch queue in the canteen, or to take the visitors along with him. This does not mean that he considers them to be of low status. It is emphasizing that he is part of the whole and that the visitor, too, if he later becomes a client, will also be a part of it.

Although some companies these days have more of a feeling for style and decorum, anyone visiting a government body or some other not-for-profit organization is certain to receive such a welcome. It has absolutely nothing to do with how important or not they consider the visitor to be. This only becomes apparent during the discussions and in the agreements made afterwards. Once these have been committed to writing, they are sacrosanct. Informal deals or casual promises have little validity and no one can appeal to them later. This means that the Dutch sometimes find themselves in trouble in societies where verbal agreements carry more weight than written ones. It can lead to disappointment for both sides.

Foreigners working in the Netherlands may often have the impression that a lot of time is wasted on talking, without it producing any results. Meetings are frequently organized for the purpose of *overleg*, consultation. There are documents to be discussed and a formal agenda. The meeting has a chairman. But the discussions rarely lead to any decisions being taken. Everyone present gives their opinions to which the others respond. This can sometimes occur in a very verbose fashion, with certain participants 'hogging the floor', while others barely say a word. At the end everyone gets out their agendas to fix a date for the next meeting. It is also quite common for the chairman to summarize the entire discussion before closing the meeting.

Anyone who misses one of these meetings because of more urgent business elsewhere does so at their peril. Even though his colleagues will quickly agree that there are far too many meetings. But the interaction that occurs is essential to the progress of the meeting. Failure to attend is seen as a sign that you do not consider the meeting or the participants important enough. This will particularly be the case if the other participants are junior to you in the organization. Absentees are quickly labelled as loners, by no means a compliment in a Dutch workplace. A loner is anathema to the belief that results depend on a team effort, rather than on any particular individual. Loners will also find themselves with a problem because they will have missed the essential information that emerged during the meeting.

At the meeting the participants will have given their standpoints on the issues under discussion and expressed their understanding for the objections and criticisms of their colleagues. By doing this, they are in a certain way responsible for any decisions made. This is known in Dutch as *meedenken*, a small word which literally means 'thinking together' but encapsulates far more. The participants in the meeting will make suggestions, without going as far as to make full-scale amendments or impose instructions. The chairman's

summaries are intended to emphasize this. This is why chairmen can often be heard to make use of certain stock expressions that express unity, such as 'We are all thinking along the same lines' or even, to translate literally, 'Our noses are once again all pointing in the same direction'.

Meetings like this are a mine of important information to enthusiastic newcomers. They can observe who has influence in the organization, and in what way. These are rarely the ones who have the most to say. If you pay close attention you will see that there are always one or two participants who only have to say a few words and the discussion on that particular point is closed. They are the people that everyone listens to.

Thanks to this *overleg*, which seems at first glance to be so time-consuming and senseless, colleagues become better attuned to each other. The time 'wasted' in meetings is recouped over and again by increased efficiency and effort in the workplace. The statistics show this very clearly. In terms of productivity, Dutch employees are among the best in the world.

Because everyone only considers an idea to be anything to do with them if they have been involved in its creation, it is advisable to take account of this when drawing up plans. Anyone submitting a finely polished proposal will see that all those involved will want a part of it. They will ask questions and make suggestions. That is why the Dutch will rarely present something as the one and only solution. They will wrap the essence of the proposal in an extra few layers in the hope that it will emerge from the discussion intact. The advantage of the consultation approach is that the discussion often produces good suggestions for improvement. And later, the plan will

no longer be yours but everybody's and you will be able to count on their full support.

HARMONIOUS RELATIONS

This strategy applies not only at 'local' level, but also on a larger scale. Dutch industry has traditionally been characterized by harmonious relations. One expression of this is the legislation which obliges companies to set up a works council made up of elected representatives of the workforce. The council does not have very extensive powers, and can do little more than advise the management. But the latter is obliged under the law to ask for that advice in specific cases, such as reorganizations or large investments. In this way, the law forces the management to consult with the representatives of the workers before making important decisions. You would expect this to bring capital and labour into conflict, but this only happens if the parties do not play by the rules. The legislation is very clear on this point. The council should have as its guiding principle the interests of the company and not of the employees it represents. Sensible managements place great value on this form of consultation. They know that the works council is an additional source of information to that provided by the middle management. It is interesting and valuable from a business point of view to see the organization from a number of different perspectives.

Relations between employers' organizations and trade unions are also very harmonious. Strikes are very rare in the Netherlands. The worst that usually happens is that one of the parties may leave the room during talks on salary increases. After a small concession, the meeting usually continues. This also has a lot to do with the role

Colleagues become better attuned to each other. The time 'wasted' in meetings is recouped over and again by increased efficiency and effort in the workplace. The statistics show this very clearly. In terms of productivity, Dutch employees are among the best in the world.

of work in the psychological makeup of the Dutch. Work for them is not something unpleasant that you have to do to earn a living. Having a paid job is an essential part of their persona. There is a general feeling that you cannot develop fully as a person if you are unemployed. Being without a job to a certain extent places you outside of society, and the consequences are described in such terms. Unemployment is the most prominent feature of social exclusion, which is so feared and seen as a major threat to the entire community. The reward for work consists therefore not just of money, but also of spiritual satisfaction and the feeling of being significant in some way. Dutch Nobel prize-winner Jan Tinbergen once suggested in a tongue-in-cheek utopian article that the two forms of reward should be inversely proportionate. Those who do dirty, unpleasant or lonely work should therefore be paid higher salaries than others whose jobs brought them into contact with a rich and varied net-work of contacts. Consequently, shoemakers would be better paid than managing directors. This, of course, would never work in practice. In fact, in recent decades the distribution of income has be-come even more unequal. But few Dutch readers of Tinbergen missed the egalitarian purity of his argument.

Negotiations between employers and employees therefore do not cover only salaries and working conditions. Other aspects are equally as important. It is not unusual for unions to make conces-

sions to help preserve or create jobs. In 1979, when the oil crisis seemed to have pulled the mat out from under the feet of the Dutch economy, bankruptcies were rife and unemployment soared, employers' organizations and trade unions – under the watchful eye of the government – reached a wide-ranging framework agreement. The employees were prepared to moderate their pay demands, and even accept a drop in their purchasing power, if the employers pledged to do their best to preserve jobs. Parties on the left and right of the political spectrum united behind the slogan of 'Work before wages'. As a consequence, the Netherlands was able to restore its competitive position within a few years. The process was not, however, without its victims. The crisis was not purely conjunctural, but also structural. Important areas of industry, such as shipping, were no longer commercially viable, which demanded large-scale restructuring programmes and great sacrifices. At the same time, the government was faced with a massive financing deficit, which was only brought down to manageable proportions little by little through consistent cutbacks in government spending.

MODERATE PAY CLAIMS

When, in the second half of the 1990s, the economic recovery started to take on the characteristics of an old fashioned boom, the trade unions tried to encourage their members to continue to moder-

ate their pay claims, because they still found work more important than wages. And, even though all the economic indicators met the requirements for participation in the EU's Economic and Monetary Union, the government continued to make cutbacks on spending. They preferred to spend the extra resources that now became available on large-scale investments, for example national transport infrastructure. The left-of-centre parties also wanted to allocate more money to what is known in the Netherlands as 'the underside of society', guaranteeing the most deprived groups a minimum standard of living.

The amount of money that the Netherlands spends on social services has always been a matter of political and, at times, fierce public debate. But the basic principle is never brought into dispute. Anyone who, through no fault of their own, is unable to support themselves, has a right to financial assistance from the community. This has sometimes led to the Netherlands having a reputation abroad as a paradise for those too lazy to work. This is far from the truth. People who draw social security benefits have an obligation to apply for jobs and the authorities ensure that they do so. Particularly in recent years, all kinds of schemes have been set up to help people get paid work, including training courses and the creation of government-funded jobs for those who are difficult to employ. The idea behind this latter scheme is that the experience will increase their employability so that they can move on to better paid work.

Does this mean that the government is taking on the responsibilities of individual citizens? There are enough economic liberals in the Netherlands who think that the system is still too generous and paternalistic. But they are preaching to increasingly empty halls. The average Dutch person is too concerned about security. The Netherlands has the highest percentage of savings of all industrial countries. And the country is a paradise for insurance companies. There are few risks that cannot be insured against and most people have policies in their desk drawers to cover every eventuality from the cradle to the grave, from fire insurance to student grants for the children, in case the government no longer has the funds to pay for them in 20 or so years' time. This natural caution has made some pension funds – you can hear young people in their 20s talking about their pensions – into leading players on the international investment markets.

All this seems to be in contradiction with the spirit of the age. The 1990s are, after all, a time of uncertainty. The old division of the world into two competing power blocs no longer exists. The revolution in information and communication technology has introduced a new dynamism into the global economy, which either rewards or punishes the taking of risks a thousand fold, while playing safe at best leads to disaster. You can try to build protective

dykes around your society to try and hold back the consequences of these developments, but they will never stand against the waves of globalization.

This belief is widespread among the Dutch. Even in radical left circles, there is a conviction that there is little point in trying to protect society from the new economic revolution. The people of the Netherlands know better than any other what you can and cannot do with a dyke. But that does not mean that they are prepared to settle for insecurity. More and more people are being forced to seek their personal security in other ways. It is not yet clear what form this will finally take, which is why good economic news is often accompanied by a feeling of pessimism. This is not surprising. In the heyday of the first big boom – the fifties and sixties – Dutch workers often stayed at the same company all their working lives. Such perseverance was seen as a great virtue, proven by the fact that forty years of loyal service to the same employer was certain to lead to a Royal honour. This automatic form of reward was abolished a few years ago, and was seen as a clear sign from the government that times had changed and the country had changed with them. These changes are reflected in the unemployment figures. Now that the 1979 recession has finally been overcome, the number of jobs is climbing steadily, but no longer at the larger companies. It is medium and small enterprises that are now creating jobs, while the large concerns are scrapping them as machines take over more and more tasks. This trend is very clear in the port of Rotterdam. 20 or 30 years ago, the port was swarming with dock-workers. Now the containers are loaded onto remote-controlled trucks. The number of people working in the port has fallen drastically, and those that remain operate computer-controlled equipment.

FLEXIBILITY

The question now is whether someone practising a single profession on the basis of a specific course of education will be able to earn a living for their entire working life. The twenty-first century demands less perseverance and more flexibility in that respect, otherwise you place yourself outside the market. And that will make you just as much of a museum piece as the steam engines that so many people lovingly restore in their free time and show off to the public on festive occasions.

In addition, employers are becoming more reluctant to employ

Foreigners who come into contact with Dutch companies – either as customers or as employees – are often confused. They are amazed at the informal way in which top-level managers and those lower down the scale interact. Secretaries address their bosses by their first names. There is little to suggest that the organization has a hierarchy. The managers' offices are simply furnished, as are the reception areas for visitors. It is not at all abnormal for the boss to join the lunch queue in the canteen, or to take the visitors along with him.

people on a permanent basis. There is an increasing tendency to take them on for specific projects, the duration and scale of which are very clearly defined. This makes the ties between employer and employee less binding. Already it is seen as a negative factor on your curriculum vitae – especially if you are applying for a higher paid job – if you have been with the same employer for too long. In the top echelons of industry, mobility has become the order of the day. Cor Boonstra, former Chairman of the Philips Board of Directors, crossed over from the packaged food industry. Gerlach Cerfontaine, Director of Schiphol Airport, who was appointed in 1998, has a medical background. Before moving to Schiphol, he was in charge of the Academic Hospital in Utrecht.

What all this means is that, even those who do not chose to run their own companies, still find themselves at the mercy of market forces. They are no longer protected from the unpredictable movements of the invisible hand, because jobs are no longer for life and skills quickly lose their relevance. Anyone who wishes to acquire some form of security in such a situation, must ensure that they possess skills which employers are prepared to pay for. That means lifelong learning, and not necessarily continually building on what you learned at school, but branching out in completely new directions.

That makes it risky to accept some kinds of work. If a certain job will not look good on your c.v., or if your employer does not give you sufficient opportunity to study further and be creative, then it will eventually become irrelevant for the flexible labour market. Workers in the Netherlands, particularly those of the younger generation, are becoming increasingly aware of this. Any company wishing to take on good, flexible employees, must make a positive contribution to their career perspectives, especially outside the organization. Otherwise, the more talented applicants will look elsewhere. This makes an innovative mentality in a company an important term of employment. Meanwhile insurance companies are developing new products to satisfy the unabated need of 'flexi-workers' for security. One consequence of this trend is that people have become job-hoppers and companies are finding it increasingly difficult to get them to stay for any length of time.

All of these developments are still in full swing. Dutch society is in the middle of a far-reaching process of transformation and adaptation. In the midst of this process it is trying to withstand the pressure of globalization and economic revolution and find a way to retain its identity. These are exciting times.

They will usually be sitting in a large circle and it will be clear, even from a distance, that there are several animated conversations going on. The table will be full of beer or wine glasses. This is a form of social interaction that the Dutch refer to with the untranslatable word '*gezelligheid*'.

JUST ACT NORMALLY, THAT'S CRAZY ENOUGH

If you take an evening stroll through an average residential district in the Netherlands, you don't have to worry about it getting dark. The streets are well lit and, if the authorities forget a corner or alleyway here or there, local residents will soon insist on these being illuminated, too.

Many of the houses also throw light out onto the street. Most Dutch houses, particularly those built after the Second World War, have large windows and the curtains are often drawn only when the occupants go to bed. Passers-by have a clear view of the many lamps that flood the room with light, and the blue flicker of the television screen. It is as though the Dutch like to make a public show of their private lives – which may come as a surprise to visitors who find them so reserved, even unfriendly. In business meetings they will come straight to the point rather than try to make any personal contact level first. They will appear to show absolutely no interest in their guests and any attempt in this direction by the latter will generally be met with total incomprehension. This attitude becomes

even more marked if the meeting is a success. After the contract has been signed, your Dutch host might invite you to join him in a drink, but that will be all. Although they tend to like working breakfasts or lunches, the food will always be simple, so as not to distract from the business at hand. So why do they offer anyone who happens to be passing a full and unimpeded view of the inside of their home – even if it is at some distance?

The passer-by will notice that the interiors of the houses have been furnished with some care. Although the furnishings will of course be more expensive in some districts than others, it is clear that the occupants have given a great deal of thought to what they want in their living rooms and are prepared, within the restrictions

of their budget, to spend a lot of money on it. Of course, the Dutch saying *Over smaak valt niet te twisten* – there's no accounting for taste – comes to mind in this context. A large number of Dutch people clearly like their houses full of bric-a-brac. A love of solid oak furniture is often accompanied by a fanatic desire to collect china, figurines and trinkets, so that the living room looks more like a gift shop. At the other end of the spectrum, there are those who prefer a carefully studied emptiness. The furniture is trendy and ultra-modern, and is kept to a minimum. But the result still radiates a feeling of comfort.

Most interiors fall somewhere between these two extremes. The evening stroller will recognize a wide variety of styles. There are certain limits to the creativity of the occupants and, although each window will present a unique picture, it will be comprised of readily available articles. Unless the walk passes through a city centre which has been colonized by wild young artists, there will be little evidence of eccentricity.

Many Dutch and foreign commentators have speculated on why the country's curtains are left wide open on dark evenings. Some claim that the occupants wish to show the world how prosperous they are. But this would be completely at variance with other aspects of the Dutch character. A second observation is perhaps nearer the truth. People want to show that they are individuals, but within certain clearly defined limits. They are saying to the passer-by: *Wij doen normaal, dan doen we gek genoeg* – we are acting normally, that's crazy enough. This may appear to contradict other principles of social life in the Netherlands. But the Dutch do not like to give offence. *Een ander in zijn waarde laten*, roughly equivalent to the English expression 'live and let live', is considered a great social virtue and a way of avoiding conflict.

NO RELIGIOUS GROUPING HAS THE UPPER HAND

This attitude, too, is deeply rooted in the country's history. It is connected to the radical divisions which have been part of Dutch society for many centuries. In this case, it is not a matter of political differences, but of religious or ideological conviction. There has never been a dominant religion in the Netherlands. Even though the majority of the people embraced Protestantism in the days of the Republic, it was practised in many different forms. In addition, there was a significant Catholic minority and several other religious communities, such as Lutherans, Baptists and Jews. None of these groupings was powerful enough to impose its norms and values on the entire community. Any religious leaders with ambitions in that direction were kept far from positions of power by the civil authorities. The Netherlands was the business emporium of Europe and intolerance of others' beliefs was bad for business. The upper classes therefore may have been practising Protestants, but they kept their distance from any form of fanaticism.

This led to a unique form of political and social development in the Netherlands during the industrial revolution. The forward march of industry and modern business in the last quarter of the nineteenth century was accompanied by a severe crisis in the rural areas. The price of food produce fell sharply as a consequence of large-scale imports from America, hitting farmers in the Netherlands very badly. There was a massive migration from the country to the cities, where rapidly expanding industry provided plenty of jobs. In a 25-year period, the populations of cities like Rotterdam, Amsterdam, The Hague and Utrecht increased three or fourfold, unleashing a gigantic social and cultural revolution. People who were accustomed to the familiar life of a small village community found themselves in amongst the gas lights of the big city. The city offered great opportunities, as could be seen in the windows of the new luxury stores and the well dressed ladies and gentlemen who were given such an elegant welcome by the store assistants. But at the same time, it was threatening and dangerous. The traditional networks of the countryside were gone, and all that mattered – or so it appeared – was money. And those who penetrated deeper into the city centres could not avoid the impression that sin was rewarded and virtue punished. With little to hold on to in the modern capitalist city, the newcomers needed something to give them a solid foundation beneath their feet. Something to stop them from sinking into this chaotic urban sea for good.

In such situations, it is natural to hold on tightly to one's deepest convictions. And in the last quarter of the nineteenth century, these were still essentially religious. The first political and social figure to really understand this was the preacher Abraham Kuyper. Originally from an upper class family from the provincial fishing town of Maassluis, Kuyper had emerged at university as a free-thinking – or as it was termed at the time, modern – theologian. But during his first assignment as a preacher, in a small village in the Betuwe region where Calvin's strict teachings were still followed to the letter, he developed into a fervent defender of the orthodox faith. And it was in this faith that Kuyper found the anchor that was missing in the rapidly changing society of the late nineteenth century. Many of Kuyper's critics accused him of a reactionary desire to return to a past when everything was better. He and his rapidly expanding group of followers were known as 'snuffers', who wanted to snuff out the candle of liberalism and progress. But Kuyper was a very modern man. He set up a newspaper to make his views available to the general public and in 1879 founded the first modern political party, the Anti-Revolutionary Party. This remarkable name was intended to illustrate his rejection of the liberalism which he saw as the child of the French Revolution. He supported the Calvinist trade union movement, and the setting up of a national network of schools, culminating in the foundation in 1880 of the Free University, still a renowned institute of further education today. In other words, Kuyper taught that the Bible, interpreted literally as Calvin insisted, was an excellent guide through the perils of modern industrial society. Anyone who sees many similarities with the various forms of fundamentalism that are currently rife, particularly in parts of the Third World, would not be mistaken.

Others followed Kuyper's example and offered programmes based on their own particular beliefs. The Catholics found their own leader in the form of the priest Herman Schaepman, while former preacher Ferdinand Domela Nieuwenhuis became the first great propagandist for socialism. Although the latter was a political doctrine, it took on many of the traits of a religion in the Netherlands – albeit a religion without a God.

None of these groupings ever had a serious chance of gaining the support of the majority of the Dutch people. They co-existed, and they needed a joint *modus vivendi*. Again it was Abraham Kuyper who first defined this need clearly. During his opening speech at the Free University, he introduced the concept of '*Souvereiniteit in eigen kring*', to be a 'prince in one's own domain'. Religious freedom, he knew, had always been one of the cornerstones of Dutch society since it had shaken off the yoke of Spanish rule under Philip II. The government had a duty to guarantee this freedom, but not through a kind of disinterested tolerance. It should actively support the religious groupings that made up Dutch society in the observance of

their faith. The primary method of providing this support was to fund religious education for the various groups. 'A prince in your own domain' therefore also meant that Kuyper's followers should be free to express the individuality of their own beliefs. And the same right applied to the Catholics and the socialists. The leaders of the groupings should work together to provide a unified national government, while the House of Orange symbolized unity within all this diversity.

In the 1960s, political scientist Arend Lijphart coined a name for this system: 'pillarization'. Dutch society, he said, was like a large building resting on a series of pillars, each rooted deeply in the ground and at some distance from each other. Together the pillars held up the entire roof. In practice, modernization in the Netherlands had occurred just as Kuyper had described. Dutch society was indeed characterized by great diversity. Complex organizational networks co-existed, for the Protestants, the Catholics, the socialists and a fourth variant loosely based on liberalism. The media, the education system, trade unions, health care and even sport were organized along these lines. The Roman Catholic Goat Breeder's Association was a frequently cited illustration of the extent to which pillarization had penetrated Dutch daily life.

One consequence of this situation was that the authorities – national, provincial and local – tended to steer clear of any form of social service that might be connected with the religious convictions of the individual. This was certainly the case in health care, and in the setting up of savings banks. The only intervention that the authorities permitted themselves in these areas was financial. The leaders of the various pillars, working together in government and parliament, set up a system of subsidies to support the activities of their members. The support was dependent on certain neutral criteria being met, such as the training of teachers or medical staff, but that was as far as it went. As a result of these efforts, a very powerful and complex network of organizations emerged in the Netherlands based on religious or ideological conviction. This network became known as the 'social midfield', the Dutch variant of the modern concept of civil society. These organizations retain their power today although, in most cases, the religious or ideological underpinnings have been eroded.

A system based on such variety can work only if everyone involved is prepared to consult with each other and to make compromises. This requires a genuine respect for other forms of belief, which can lead to a certain restraint in one's conduct. A perfect example of this is sport on Sundays. Until recently, Protestants had serious objections to the playing of sports on the Lord's day of rest.

Catholics, socialists and liberals did not share these objections, but organized the competitions on Sunday afternoons so that Protestants going to church in the mornings would not be confronted with people on their way to the sports clubs. Conversely, Protestant politicians did not boycott coalitions with Catholics even though the latter refused to cooperate on a ban on funfairs, a sinful pastime in the eyes of Calvin's followers. Sometimes, this caution went a little too far. In the early years of this century, Calvinist Amsterdam Mayor De Vlugt wanted to ban a play which depicted the arrival of Jesus Christ in modern-day London, because he was afraid that it would offend the Catholics. Priest and journalist Hyacinth Hermans, leading light in the prominent daily paper *De Maasbode*, succeeded in persuading De Vlugt that his fellow Catholics were actually deeply impressed by the message of the play.

In other words, in your own domain, you can be consistent and unwilling to compromise, but outside you should adopt a low profile. You do not give offence, because others do not offend you.

YOU HAVE THE RIGHT TO BE YOURSELF.
As in the rest of Europe, the enormous wave of prosperity in the second half of this century set in motion a far-reaching process of secularization in the Netherlands. Although most Dutch people will admit to believing in 'something' and may feel a vague bond with one religious grouping or another, the number of regular churchgoers has fallen drastically. Genuine orthodox communities are to be found only among the smaller Protestant churches and a Catholic minority. Altogether they amount to less than 18,000 souls. The religious press has had to widen its horizons or go under, while the Christian political parties have seen their share of the vote shrink from more than half to just over a fifth. But the mentality that characterized the pillarized society remains intact. No one wants to give offence, but at the same time everyone has the right to be a prince in their own domain. The pillars have now been replaced by subcultures. Some people may belong to several, widely varying subcultures. It is important to keep the norms, values and rules of the different groups separate, or you may find yourself in trouble. Anyone who goes to a sado-masochistic Wasteland party – as thousands of people do – would be well-advised to leave the Armani suit and the image that goes with it at home, or they will not get past the door. Inside, rubber, leather, patent and chains are the order of the day. It is very probable that the slave girl chained to the bar will change into her casual weekend clothes at the end of the party and go to visit her family, while during the week she dons a suit and takes part in the endless meetings that go with her demanding job

at City Hall. Or she may be a salsa dancer, or a keen sports woman. The principle of being a prince in your own domain has been transferred from the old pillars to a modern tolerance of different lifestyles. Here, too, the motto is 'live and let live'.

This is not to say that the Dutch do not like to look over the hedge and see what the neighbours are doing. But they will do it at a discreet distance. This is the reason for the popularity of television programmes devoted to conspicuous lifestyles, many of which at least appear to have thrown all norms and values to the wind. It is acceptable to show others how you live and why. But is 'not done' to force yourself upon others without invitation. After all, on the television, you can always change the channel. And, what is more important, there is no actual physical confrontation. There is a considerable distance between the viewers and the person who is displaying his or her unusual preferences, so the encounter cannot lead to open conflict. In the past, you could often see little mirrors hanging outside Dutch windows. They allowed the occupants to see who was at the door. In some ways, the television has taken over the role of these mirrors.

Are the Dutch really as closed and introspective as this might suggest? Are they, as a well-known saying goes, afraid to 'expose themselves', except – often in a literal sense – within certain sub-cultures? Here, too, we can learn much from our evening stroll. Through some of the windows we can see very lively groups of people. Not that everyone is dancing around. They will more usually be sitting in a large circle and it will be clear, even from a distance, that there are several animated conversations going on. The table will be full of beer or wine glasses. This is a form of social interaction that the Dutch refer to with the untranslatable word '*gezelligheid*'. You cannot be happy unless your life contains a large dose of *gezelligheid*. A little etymology may help to bring us closer to the true significance of this interaction. '*-heid*' is a suffix that usually indicates a situation. '*Gezel*' is an old word that originally meant something like 'partner' or 'friend'. A *levensgezel*, for example, is one's 'life partner', and is a traditional synonym for spouse.

The essential feature of anything that is *gezellig* is friendship. For the Dutch friendship stands outside the normal circuits of business and public life. Among friends there is no need for continual negotiation and compromise. The relationship is based purely on personal like and respect and there are no competing interests to take into account. It is therefore not at all unusual for political opponents who attack each other viciously in parliamentary debates to be close friends, to be seen together at the bar or to be regular visitors to visit each other's houses. This may also be true of business rivals.

The Dutch want to show that they are individuals, but within certain clearly defined limits. They are saying to the passer-by: *Wij doen normaal, dan doen we gek genoeg* – we are acting normally, that's crazy enough. This may appear to contradict other principles of social life in the Netherlands. But the Dutch do not like to give offence. *Een ander in zijn waarde laten*, roughly equivalent to the English expression 'live and let live', is considered a great social virtue and a way of avoiding conflict.

You can, of course, expect support from your friends, but this is always in personal matters. It would disrupt the relationship to, for example, ask for a loan or for preferential treatment in a business transaction. This is to abuse the situation, and the Dutch are quick to smell the penetrating odour of corruption.

ALL TACT SEEMS TO HAVE DISAPPEARED

Anyone confronted with true Dutch *gezelligheid* for the first time is in for a great surprise. All reserve, and tact, seems to have disappeared. People who may be known for their moderate views at work might suddenly express the strongest and wildest opinions on a wide variety of issues. This will invoke equally impassioned denials. To cries of 'Nonsense!' and 'Rubbish!', the original speaker will repeat the argument twice as loudly. You would be mistaken for thinking that they were all just looking for a fight, if the conversation were not regularly interrupted by hearty laughter, or if every sarcastic comment were not greeted so enthusiastically. You might wonder if this is all a game. Far from it. Everyone is completely serious, they all mean every word they say. They are expressing their deepest convictions and are inviting you to do the same. It would not be *gezellig* if you were to refuse the offer, and restrict yourself to a superficial contribution to the discussion.

The partygoers can afford to let themselves go like this, because they are among friends. The main criterion for *gezelligheid* is that the situation is not threatening for anyone and that no consequences are drawn from what is said. From time to time, journalists will quote something that has been said at an informal gathering. This always leads to trouble. They have confused business and pleasure, and shown a lack of respect for privacy. In doing so they have forfeited the rights of friendship in the eyes of those involved and the general public.

But there are limits to this *gezelligheid*, not all barriers can be cast aside. No matter how much tempers may rise – about burning social or political issues, for example – no one is permitted to make personal remarks about the character or integrity of anyone present. The *gezelligheid* would rapidly turn into hostility. Not that a fight would break out, nor would the offender be shown the door. He or she would simply be ignored and excluded from further participation in the conversation. And the next time, there is a good chance that the violator of the unwritten laws of *gezelligheid* would simply not be invited.

If you want to make friends in the Netherlands you should make a clear distinction between business and public contacts, and your private social life. The Dutch tend to meet their friends at clubs or in the cafe. Because they do not like to talk to outsiders about their personal circumstances and consider questions about themselves to show a lack of respect, conversations with people they have just met usually avoid such topics and are restricted to neutral ground, such as football, a shared hobby, holidays, good restaurants or that old favourite, the weather, about which the Dutch always have something to say. If this introductory conversation should lead to sufficient mutual like and respect, a friendship may develop. Once it does, it will be very close. This is what makes Dutch society both very open and very closed. Everyone is permitted to choose their own lifestyle, but that does make it difficult to establish close relationships. The problem is that the various forms of contact between these two extremes, which offer an effective remedy for loneliness in many other cultures, do not exist in the Netherlands. This is very clearly visible in the country's parks. If someone can choose between a bench that is occupied and one that is already being used, they will invariably choose the empty one. At bus stops, there is a stony silence, except between people who know each other. There is a Dutch expression that describes this mentality. They say that it is difficult to establish contact, but that it is all much easier once 'the ice is broken'. The ice metaphor speaks volumes, but most Dutch people will admit to a preference to take their holidays in countries where the local people are approachable and easy to talk to. It is as if they get the *gezelligheid* for nothing and without having to make a special effort.

In the past thirty years or so, the composition of the population has changed radically. For the second time in its history, the Netherlands has become a favourite destination for many groups of immigrants. In the seventeenth century, the heyday of the Republic, countless newcomers sought a better future in the prosperous new state on the North Sea. Around 1650, almost half of the population of Amsterdam was of foreign origin. The French-speaking L'Eglise Wallone still bears witness to the fact that, several hundreds of years ago, tens of thousands of Protestant Huguenots fled persecution in their homeland to build up a new life in the Netherlands. The current wave of immigration is largely the result of the great prosperity that swept Europe after the Second World War. As a result of the rapid economic growth, by the end of the 1950s, there was a potential labour shortage. Companies were granted permission to recruit workers abroad. They started in Italy, Spain and, to a lesser extent, Portugal. Later they had to cast their nets more widely, in Morocco and the eastern part of Turkey, where unemployment was very high. The original intention was that these 'guest workers' would stay in the Netherlands temporarily and then return home

with a substantial nest egg for their families. Most of the guest workers felt the same way. Surveys showed that the majority of them dreamed of going home and setting up their own businesses.

The salaries in the Netherlands are, indeed, considerably higher than in Morocco or Turkey. But so are the prices. For most guest workers, the dream of setting up a business back at home, gradually faded into the background. While they were in the Netherlands, they accrued a number of rights, including the right to be reunited with their families. As a consequence, Turkish and Moroccan communities with a more permanent character grew up in many Dutch cities. There are now second and third generation immigrants who have grown up in the Netherlands, and who know Turkey and Morocco only from holidays and the special channels on cable television.

In addition to the Turks and Moroccans, the Netherlands has a number of other ethnic minority groups from the former colony of Suriname, on the north coast of South America, and the Caribbean islands of Curaçao, Bonaire, Aruba, Saba, Sint Maarten and Sint Eustatius, all of which are still self-governing parts of the Kingdom of the Netherlands. In addition, there are tens of thousands of Cape Verdeans in Rotterdam, while Amsterdam, and the modern district of Bijlmermeer in particular, has become a favoured destination of immigrants from Ghana. The preference for the Netherlands in Ghana may have something to do with the fact that Dutch colonists only left the country in 1871. A last minority group of significance comes from Indonesia, also a former Dutch colony.

All of these groups bear witness to the fact that the Netherlands was once a prominent colonial power. The basis for this was laid in the Golden Age, when two companies set up with government support were responsible for trade outside Europe. The United East India Company operated in Asia, while its sister company, the West India Company, was active in Africa and the Americas. The current generation looks back on this past with mixed feelings. Before the Second World War, school children still learned a well-known song about the Dutch flag, that contained the line: 'Zie ik Hollands vlag aan vreemde kust, dan juicht mijn hart 'victorie'' – 'When I see the flag of Holland on a far coast, my heart cries 'victory'. But today there is a vague feeling of guilt about what their forefathers did when they reached those far shores. The West India Company, for example, started to participate in the slave trade after an obliging preacher had provided a theological justification for it in a successful book entitled 'The Spiritual Rudder of the Merchant Ship'. When the Netherlands finally abolished slavery in its American colonies in 1863, it was the last European country to do so.

This is nothing to be proud of. And, as Dutch people of Caribbean origin point out, the slave trade is given very summary treatment in history teaching in schools. For some time, there have been plans in the pipeline to erect a monument to the victims of slavery. Just to give you an idea of the realities of slavery: in the eighteenth century slave traders and plantation owners could insure their human property against early death. The standard owner's risk was 15%.

Relations between the Netherlands and Indonesia continue to be coloured by the colonial past. From the very beginning, the United East India Company exercized political as well as economic power. Its main priority was always to make a profit, and this did not change

If you want to make friends in the Netherlands you should make a clear distinction between business and public contacts, and your private social life. The Dutch tend to meet their friends at clubs or in the cafe. If this introductory conversation should lead to sufficient mutual like and respect, a friendship may develop. Once it does, it will be very close.

when its responsibilities were taken over by the Dutch government. The Dutch East Indies were expected to yield considerable revenue, and around 1850, the colony was almost single-handedly responsible for the healthy state of the national budget. In fact, the modernization of the infrastructure necessary for the industrial revolution was largely financed by income from the East Indies. How did this work? The colonial government forced local farmers to grow certain crops, such as coffee and sugar, as a form of taxation, which were then sold in Europe at high prices. The products were sold by auction in Amsterdam. The fact that the farmers were unable to grow sufficient food to feed their families was hardly taken into account.

TAKEN, NOT GIVEN

This system was abolished in the nineteenth century and replaced by a policy of economic liberalism, that gave European investors the opportunity to exploit the riches of the colony. In addition, the Royal Netherlands Indies Army waged a cruel campaign to ensure that the authority of the colonial power extended to all corners of the enormous complex of islands. It was, however, not all exploitation and repression. In 1899 Conrad van Deventer, a well-known expert on the East Indies, wrote a magazine article that caused immediate uproar. In the article, entitled *Een Ereschuld*, A Debt of Honour, Van Deventer claimed that the Netherlands had taken its colonies, but never given anything back. That created an obligation which, could be fulfilled through a strategy that was practically identical to what we would these days call development policy. The ultimate aim was to teach the Indonesians how to be self-sufficient. In this respect, Van Deventer had not entirely shaken off his Western feelings of superiority. Subsequently, the colonial government began to present itself as an educator. At the same time, however, it refused to accept the Indonesian nationalist movement as a serious discussion partner. In the opinion of Hendrikus Colijn, an anti-revolutionary politician who headed several cabinets in the 1930s, it would take three hundred years to educate the Indonesians to the required level. When the Netherlands and Indonesia finally parted company, it was a traumatic farewell. In the Second World War, the Japanese overran the colony with little difficulty. When they surrendered after Hiroshima, the Indonesian leaders Sukarno and Hatta declared the new republic of Indonesia. The Netherlands did not recognize it and sent an expeditionary force, not so much to restore colonial rule as to ensure that independence took the desired form. The conflict escalated into a cruel colonial war, that came to end only after the major powers, with the United States at the forefront, forced the Nether-

lands to step back. In 1949, after negotiations in Amsterdam, the Netherlands recognized Indonesian independence.

This episode in Dutch history is also nothing to be proud of and the current generation generally distance themselves from the actions of their forefathers in this respect. All the former colonial heroes and conquerors have well and truly fallen from the pedestals of the monuments that still stand in their memory around the country. And yet it is accurate to speak of a historical trauma. Certain important parts of the Netherlands' colonial past do not fit in with the Dutch self-image of a small, democratic and peace-loving nation. Public opinion is still shocked from time to time by new revelations about the not too distant past that dent this image. They always lead to agitation in the media and to a communal attack of guilt. This feeling of unease is one of the fundaments of modern development cooperation, which is also considered sacrosanct by politicians across the board. It allows you to show that you have changed. Whether that is how the recipients always experience it in practice is a different matter.

However you see it, the colonial past is partly responsible for much of the multicultural nature of modern Dutch society. This is discernible not only in the wide variety of international dishes available in restaurants, even in the smallest towns and villages, but also in the extent to which cultural events from around the world are becoming a prominent part of the Dutch entertainments calendar. One of the most spectacular examples of this is the Antillean Summer Carnival in Rotterdam, which is threatening to replace London's Notting Hill Carnival as Europe's most renowned multicultural festival. And there is the Pasar Malam, a covered market in The Hague, where an Indonesian ideal becomes a reality for a few days. But these events are surpassed, at least in scale and numbers, by the annual Dunya Festival in Rotterdam. Dunya means 'world' in Arabic, Turkish and Indonesian. It has its roots in the annual Poetry International festival, which attracts poets from around the world. In the 1970s they had the idea of organizing performances in a park in the city. This evolved into a gigantic multicultural event which now attracts hundreds of thousands of visitors. An increasing number of Dutch towns are organizing smaller scale versions of the Dunya festival. They all provide visitors with the opportunity to show that they are no longer guilty of the patterns of behaviour that typified the colonial era. Their traditional attitude of colonial superiority has been superseded by a genuine appreciation of other cultures, of what they see on offer at the festivals. And that gives the modern Dutch man or woman a good feeling.

The major cities now also have an international, multicultural flavour. You will see more and more minarets among the church towers, as Islam has become the country's second largest religion after Christianity. Where there are communities of Hindus – who have generally arrived in the Netherlands after a double wave of migration; their forefathers left India for Suriname in the nineteenth century – you will find Hindu temples. And in the Bijlmermeer, more and more parking garages are being converted into Christian churches with an African character.

MULTICULTURAL LOVE IS WIDESPREAD

In the 1980s a serious public debate developed around the integration of these minority groups. The debate has had a particularly Dutch character. In view of the national tradition, integration cannot mean giving up your specific background and culture to become part of a unified national mass. Abraham Kuyper in effect ruled that out more than a century ago. The first measure that the government took for these newcomers was to organize courses on a grand scale, not in the Dutch language and culture but in that of their own countries, so that it was not lost. The thought that these immigrants would eventually return to their home countries was another reason for providing these courses.

This policy has since been changed. In spite of the multinational character of the street scene, particularly in the country's major cities, Dutch language, culture and customs are still completely dominant. Anyone who is unable to function in Dutch surroundings, or whose command of Dutch is insufficient for them to express themselves, particularly in writing, will encounter problems at school and in pursuing a career. Furthermore, discrimination and prejudice are not uncommon, in spite of their being forbidden under the Dutch constitution – the article concerned is engraved in a monument outside the parliament buildings. These days, the government enters into a contract with new immigrants. The newcomers pledge to follow courses in the Dutch language and culture, which the state in its turn undertakes to provide for them.

This produces a sort of balance – or, at least, this is the intention. Too many statistics suggest an opposite picture. Unemployment among ethnic minority groups is far higher than among 'native' Dutch workers. And practical experience shows that the children of immigrant families have more problems at school. The more talented ones can push their way through to university without too many problems, but the more average pupils too frequently encounter problems developing their potential to the full in primary and secondary schools. It is a something of a consolation that the government sees this as an urgent social problem.

On the other hand, the small and medium-size enterprise sector in the major cities is gradually taking on a more multicultural character. Immigrants have introduced services hitherto unknown in the Netherlands, such as take-out meals delivered to the home. When it became clear that minorities could become trend-setters, they were discovered by marketeers and advertizing agencies. While the Dutch initially responded sceptically to the cell phone – *doe gewoon, dan doe je gek genoeg* – minority groups enthusiastically em-braced this new means of communication. The business sector is also starting to discover these new consumer groups, and that is good for integration.

Figures from the Central Planning Bureau suggest another trend in this direction. Fifteen percent of marriages in the Netherlands each year are now between partners of different nationalities. This confirms the suspicion that multicultural love is becoming widespread. A development that gives rise to hope that the current tensions are not long-lasting. If the members of the different cultural groups are not only doing more business together, but are also kissing and cuddling a lot more often, the future will be a lot more harmonious.

COLOPHON

COPYRIGHT © SCRIPTUM PUBLISHERS

PHOTOGRAPHY FREEK VAN ARKEL GEORGE BURGGRAAFF BEN DEIMAN

ETIENNE VAN SLOUN | GREGOR RAMAEKERS KAREL TOMEÏ

TEXT HAN VAN DER HORST

TRANSLATION ANDY BROWN

DESIGN AND LAYOUT PAUL WEIJS

LITHOGRAPHY AND PRINTING SNOECK-DUCAJU & ZOON

ISBN 90 5594 114 X

1

BURGGRAAFF A 'low sky' in Beesd, Gelderland

2

BURGGRAAFF Pigs in a stall, Valkenswaard, Noord-Brabant

4

BURGGRAAFF Clog market in Doetinchem, Gelderland

6

BURGGRAAFF Young calves, Bolsward, Friesland

18

TOMEÏ, Polder at Rietwijk, Kedichem, Zuid-Holland

20

SLOUN│RAMAEKERS Field cross set in the hilly Limburg landscape
TOMEÏ River Geul, Limburg

22

TOMEÏ Hilly landscape near Vaals, Limburg

24

SLOUN│RAMAEKERS River Maas near Eijsden, Limburg

34

TOMEÏ, Sambeek lock, Limburg and Krammer lock, Zeeland

36

BURGGRAAFF River Berkel near Borculo, Gelderland

38

BURGGRAAFF The Neder Rijn near Rhenen, Utrecht

40

TOMEÏ Cornfields in the Noordoostpolder, Flevoland

50

BURGGRAAFF Fruit auction in the Westland district of Zuid-Holland

52

TOMEÏ Cabbage field, Nieuw-Vennep, N-Holland
BURGGRAAFF Sugar beet, tomatoes, mushrooms, lettuce, endive, plums and onions

54

BURGGRAAFF Tulips, Vogelenzang, Noord-Holland

56

TOMEÏ Greenhouses in the Westland region of Zuid-Holland
BURGGRAAFF Greenhouses (detail)

66

TOMEÏ Farms in the Noordoostpolder, Flevoland and Middelharnis, Zeeland

68

TOMEÏ Flax harvest, Zeeuws-Vlaanderen and grain harvest, Noord-Beveland, Zeeland

70

TOMEÏ Fruit pickers near Tiel, Gelderland
TOMEÏ Nursery near Teuge, Gelderland

72

TOMEÏ Fruit orchard in the Betuwe region, Gelderland and flower fields near Noordwijkerhout, Zuid-Holland

10

BURGGRAAFF River Lek at Vianen, Zuid-Holland

12

BURGGRAAFF Clouds in Drenthe, Flevoland and Noord-Brabant

14

BURGGRAAFF River Waal at Dodewaard, Gelderland and Church tower at Buurmalsen, Gelderland

16

BURGGRAAFF River Waal at Haaften, Gelderland
BURGGRAAFF Cows near Klazienaveen, Drenthe

26

TOMEÏ River Maas, Limburg

28

TOMEÏ Landscape near Lopikerwaard, Utrecht

30

BURGGRAAFF Storm on the River Waal, Gameren, Gelderland

32

TOMEÏ Storm barrier in the Oosterschelde, Zeeland
BURGGRAAFF Gale force 10, Vlissingen, Zeeland

42

BURGGRAAFF Clay fields, Buren, Gelderland and packaged crops, Heiloo, Noord-Holland

44

SLOUN|RAMAEKERS Cornfields near Valkenburg, Limburg
TOMEÏ Irrigation in Flevoland

46

BURGGRAAFF Bales of hay, Zeewolde, Flevopolder
TOMEÏ Electricity pylon, Noord-Brabant

48

BURGGRAAFF Corn harvesting, Goor, Overijssel
TOMEÏ Sheaves, Tholen, Zeeland

58

TOMEÏ Flower nursery, Boskoop, Zuid-Holland

60

TOMEÏ Various crops, Belfeld, Limburg
TOMEÏ Flowers, Noordwijkerhout, Zuid-Holland

62

TOMEÏ Train passing through rape field, Flevoland and Farmland in Noord-Holland

64

TOMEÏ Cornfields near Dollard, Groningen, and on the banks of the Westerschelde, Zeeland

74

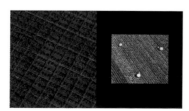

TOMEÏ Flower fields, De Zilk, Zuid-Holland and flower field with trees, near Lisse, Zuid-Holland

76

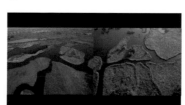

TOMEÏ Flower nursery, Utrecht
TOMEÏ Pickers under parasols, Flevoland

78

TOMEÏ Aarlanderveen, Zuid-Holland

80

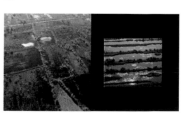

TOMEÏ Haaksbergerveen, Overijssel
TOMEÏ Rottige Meente, near Wolvega, Friesland

82

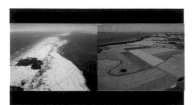

TOMEÏ The Frisian island of Terschelling after a snowfall and Groothuissenpolder, Zeeland

84

TOMEÏ Cranes at Bergeyk, Noord-Barbant

86

VAN ARKEL The Europoort industrial area, Rotterdam, Zuid-Holland

88

SLOUN│RAMAEKERS DSM, Geleen, Limburg
VAN ARKEL Power station on the Maasvlakte, Zuid-Holland

98

VAN ARKEL Container transit, Maasvlakte, Zuid-Holland

100

VAN ARKEL Mixed cargo transit, Rotterdam, Zuid-Holland

102

VAN ARKEL Industrial harbour area, Rotterdam, Zuid-Holland

104

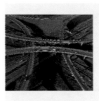

TOMEÏ Prins Clausplein motorway intersection, The Hague, Zuid-Holland
VAN ARKEL The twin Van Brienenoord bridges across the Nieuwe Maas, Rotterdam, Zuid-Holland

114

TOMEÏ Yacht race with the Zeeland bridge in the background, Zeeland

116

TOMEÏ Skating on the River Rotte, Zuid-Holland
DEIMAN Elfstedentocht, the eleven-cities skating marathon in Friesland
BURGGRAAFF Skating near Dongjum, Friesland

118

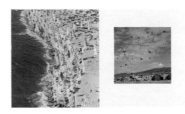

TOMEÏ Catamaran race on the island of Texel
BURGGRAAFF Flying kites on the beach, Callantsoog, Noord-Holland

120

TOMEÏ Beach, Katwijk, Noord-Holland
TOMEÏ Rock festival, Eindhoven, Noord-Brabant

130

BURGGRAAFF St. Nicholas, Buren, Gelderland

132

SLOUN│RAMAEKERS Carnival, Maastricht, Limburg

136

DEIMAN Queen's Day, Amsterdam, Noord-Holland

138

VAN ARKEL A 'Low Sky' in Hook of Holland, Zuid-Holland

90

TOMEÏ Iron storage, Beek en Donk, Noord-Brabant

92

VAN ARKEL Coal transport to Germany across the
Hartel Canal, Zuid-Holland

94

BURGGRAAFF Mussel fisherman, Oosterschelde,
Zeeland

96

VAN ARKEL Freighter and tug, Nieuwe Waterweg,
Zuid-Holland
VAN ARKEL Pilot, North Sea

106

VAN ARKEL Heavy traffic on the A13,
Rotterdam, Zuid-Holland and
Erasmus bridge, Rotterdam, Zuid-Holland

108

BURGGRAAFF Canoeing on the River Korne,
Gelderland

110

TOMEÏ Aquaduct at Roelofarendsveen,
Zuid-Holland VAN ARKEL Water sports, Kralingse
Plas, Rotterdam, Zuid-Holland

112

VAN ARKEL Rotterdam Centre, Zuid-Holland
TOMEÏ Kagerplassen near Leiden, Zuid-Holland

122

DEIMAN Vondelpark, Amsterdam, Noord-Holland

124

TOMEÏ Picnic on the River Vecht, Utrecht

126

TOMEÏ Public allotments near Amsterdam,
Noord-Brabant

128

SLOUN | RAMAEKERS Brass band, Maastricht,
Limburg